The door is open

Asahel Nettleton

EVANGELICAL PRESS

EVANGELICAL PRESS
Grange Close, Faverdale North Industrial Estate, Darlington, Co. Durham, DL3 0PH, England

The original sermons on which this booklet is based were previously published in the USA.
This edition first published 1998.

British Library Cataloguing in Publication Data available

ISBN 0 85234 409 0

Scripture quotations in this publication are from the Authorized/ King James Version.

Printed and bound in Great Britain by Bailes, Houghton-le-Spring, Tyne & Wear.

Preface

Asahel Nettleton was born on 21 April 1783 in Killingworth, Connecticut and his life spanned a period which was of crucial importance both in the establishment of the future political system of the United States of America and in the spiritual life of the nation.

Asahel was the eldest son of a New England farmer and his early upbringing prepared him to follow in his father's footsteps and become a farmer. As a boy he received the usual instruction given to young people in the Congregational church and the teaching of the Westminster catechism made a deep impression on him. Though he led an outwardly moral and upright life, he knew deep down in his heart that he had not experienced the new birth and came under deep conviction of his need to be in a right relationship with God. This continued over a period of several months until at last he found peace as he trusted in Christ alone for salvation. It was 1801 when the revival which came to be known as the Second Great Awakening first touched the community where Asahel Nettleton lived and, at the age of eighteen, he became one of the first converts of the revival in that place.

Although he continued to work on his father's farm his thoughts turned increasingly to another and greater harvest-field where labourers were needed. As he read accounts of the work being carried out by William Carey and other pioneers in the field of overseas missions, his heart was stirred with a longing to give himself to a similar work. However, any hopes he might have entertained of going to college in preparation for service overseas received a devastating setback the following year when an epidemic claimed the lives of his father and one of his younger brothers and the principal burden for the support of his family fell on Asahel's shoulders. But he never lost the vision of a college education in preparation for missionary work. In the meantime he began studying in his free time under the tuition of his local pastor and, taking advantage of the comparative quiet on the farm in the winter months, supplemented his income by employment as a teacher until in 1805 he was in a position, both academically and financially, to enrol as a student at Yale.

During his time at Yale the college and the surrounding area were touched by a further period of revival and Nettleton spent many hours counselling fellow-students who had come under a conviction of sin and were seeking peace with God. After graduating from Yale, Nettleton spent a period of time as assistant to a pastor and was formally licensed as a preacher in May 1811.

He still hoped at this stage to become a missionary overseas but it was while awaiting direction as to his future course of service that he was invited to address a meeting at the town of South Britain on 13 October 1812 en route for another preaching engagement. That meeting was to mark a turning-point in his life. He preached that day with a totally new power and unction and in the days that followed had the joy of seeing many brought to a real, living faith in Christ under the impact of his ministry. This pattern was to be repeated in other places and it soon became clear that

Nettleton's calling was to be that of an evangelist in his homeland — initially in his native Connecticut and then further afield until at the time of his death a New York newspaper could write, 'Few men, since the apostolic days, have been honoured with such signal success in preaching the word, and in the conversion of sinners as he...' Indeed, he was to emerge as the leading preacher of the period of revival which has gone down in history under the title of the Second Great Awakening. Wherever he went the power of God rested on his ministry and churches and communities were transformed as great numbers of those among whom he laboured underwent a profound and lasting experience of genuine conversion.

In 1822, almost exactly ten years after the commencement of this remarkable ministry, Nettleton contracted typhus fever and for some weeks his life was in danger. He eventually recovered and was able to resume his ministry, but he never fully regained the vigour and vitality which had characterized those early years when he was at the height of his powers. In 1838, at the age of fifty-six, he retired to East Windsor Hill in New England, where he devoted his time to reading and Bible study. He also maintained an active interest in the Theological Institute of Connecticut (later to become Hartford Theological Seminary), of which he was one of the first trustees. He died on 16 May 1844 after a protracted illness.

Nettleton's ministry combined a penetrating analysis of the human heart with faithfulness to the truths of Scripture. Although he was involved in some of the great theological controversies of his day and was closely involved in the founding of a theological seminary, it was as a preacher and soul-winner that he deserves to be remembered.

It is hoped that in presenting the three messages in this booklet in a new version for the modern reader, this preacher who was so mightily used of God in former times may once again speak powerfully to the hearts of men and women today.

Editing of the text has been limited to a minimum. In a few places it has been necessary to reconstruct the wording of a passage where the original text was fragmentary or incomplete, or where the material was presented in note form. A few archaic sentence structures and expressions have been omitted or replaced with more modern equivalents. Specific references in the text to the congregation present when these sermons were first preached have been dropped and the relevant passages amended to reflect the fact that the message is now being presented in a written form.

In addition to these changes some headings have been inserted, or the wording of the others amended to make the flow of thought within each message more immediately obvious to the reader. Nettleton's language abounds with biblical quotations and allusions, with which the reader may not always be familiar, and a number of Bible references have therefore also been inserted at appropriate points in the text to assist the reader in recognizing and understanding such passages.

Throughout the aim has been to make the preaching of Nettleton more accessible to the modern reader while retaining its original character. All Scripture quotations have been taken from the Authorized/King James Version as in the original sermons.

The publishers
March 1998

The door is open

The certain destruction of all who do not seek salvation rightly

'For many, I say unto you, will seek to enter in, and shall not be able' (Luke 13:24).

The question was put: 'Lord, are there few that be saved?' And he said to them, 'Strive to enter in at the strait gate: for many, I say unto you, will seek to enter in, and shall not be able' (Luke 13:23,24). Here is an interesting question — a question about salvation. It leads to a useful, though an alarming, answer. To the question, 'Are there few that will be saved?' mankind have given different answers. It is a question above the reach of human reason. Whether few or many, or any at all, will finally be saved are questions that cannot be determined without a revelation from God. Discarding the word of fallible mortals, we must depend upon divine revelation. We appeal to our omniscient Saviour. Whatever men may say, the Son of God has declared, 'Many, I say unto you, will seek to enter in, and shall not be able.' What proportion of the whole race of Adam will finally be saved or lost I cannot say, for I have not been told. But one thing is certain: 'Many ... will seek to enter in, and shall not be able.'

Let us attend to the fact asserted in this text.

1. Many have sought salvation and have missed it

All who exert themselves in religion do, in some sense, seek to enter heaven. Even the heathen, who know nothing of the Saviour, are concerned about a future state. They build temples, worship idols and offer sacrifices. They offer their own children in sacrifice and subject themselves to the most cruel tortures — and all for what? To atone for sin and to obtain pardon and salvation. All these exertions are demonstrations of anxiety and concern about a future state. Thousands, millions even, have sought in this manner to enter heaven, and have not been able to do so.

With respect to idolaters we have a positive declaration that they 'shall not inherit the kingdom of God' (1 Cor. 6:9). For 'Without are ... murderers, and idolaters, and whosoever loveth and maketh a lie' (Rev. 22:15).

Cain, as well as Abel, offered a sacrifice. He 'brought of the fruit of the ground an offering unto the Lord'. And the Lord had respect to the offering of the one and not of the other (Gen. 4:3-5). Both sought, and yet both were not accepted.

The Jews in the time of Isaiah offered thousands of sacrifices, appeared before the Lord in solemn assemblies and made many prayers. And yet the Lord declares, 'When ye spread forth your hands, I will hide mine eyes from you ... when ye make many prayers, I will not hear' (Isa. 1:15).

When Christ was on earth, many were punctual in all the external observances of religion. They prayed and fasted and paid tithes of all that they possessed. In this manner they sought, and yet were excluded. 'For', says the Saviour, 'I say unto you, that except your righteousness shall exceed the righteousness of the scribes and Pharisees, ye shall in no case enter into the kingdom of heaven' (Matt. 5:20).

The Jews at the present day, even though they denounce Christ as an impostor, are nevertheless punctual in observing the duties of their religion. They are seeking to enter heaven. And yet Christ told them, 'Ye shall die in your sins: for if ye believe not that I am he, ye shall die in your sins' (John 8:24).

Thus many have sought to enter heaven and have not been able to do so. These, you will remember, did not live as those who are unconcerned; they were not without thoughts on the subject of salvation.

2. This truth is evident from plain declarations of Scripture

At the Day of Judgement many will be found pleading for admittance into heaven on the grounds of their religious duties: 'Many will say to me in that day, "Lord, Lord, have we not prophesied in thy name? And in thy name cast out devils? And in thy name done many wonderful works?" And then will I profess unto them, "I never knew you: depart from me, ye that work iniquity" ' (Matt. 7:22-23).

The text itself is a sufficient confirmation of this fact: 'Many, I say unto you, will seek to enter in, and shall not be able.' You will notice that the Saviour is not speaking of those who do not, and will not, think of religion. He is not speaking of those who sit down and do nothing. But, what renders it still more alarming, he is speaking of those who seek to enter heaven. They sought and were not able to enter. They were 'not able', says Christ; but if they sought to enter, why were they not able to do so?

No doubt the reader will answer: 'Because they did not seek in the right way.' This is undoubtedly correct. Many will seek to enter heaven but will not be able to do so for the same reason. They will not seek in the right way. Everything depends on the manner of seeking. Then let us point out some of the ways in which sinners may seek, and yet miss salvation.

1. They do not seek it as a thing of first importance

The direction is: 'Seek … first the kingdom of God' (Matt. 6:33). Let it be the first and leading object of your pursuit. Everything else must give way, and lie in subordination to this object. Whatever may come in competition, however dear, you must be able to renounce it without a sigh. 'The kingdom of heaven is like unto treasure hid in a field; the which when a man hath found, he hideth, and for joy thereof goeth and selleth all that he hath, and buyeth that field' (Matt. 13:44).

But many who attend to the subject of religion will not seek it in this manner. They will attend to the subject by and by. They do not make it 'the one thing needful', nor feel its overwhelming importance. The grand maxim of many is: 'Seek first the world, and then if you can find time…' Though they attend to religion, yet they attend more to the world. All who attend to the subject in this manner will miss heaven. 'No man can serve two masters: for either he will hate the one, and love the other; or else he will hold to the one, and despise the other. Ye cannot serve God and mammon' (Matt. 6:24).

2. They seek to enter by their own righteousness

Many will trust to what they have done, to what they are doing and to what they intend to do. It will not be through want of zeal, or of being engaged in religious activities; not because they did not do more, but because they trusted in what they did. This was the fatal mistake of some in the time of the apostles: 'For I bear them record that they have a zeal of God, but not according to knowledge. For they being ignorant of God's righteousness, and going about to establish their own righteousness, have not submitted themselves unto the righteousness of God' (Rom. 10:3). They compass themselves about with sparks which they have kindled and they shall lie down in sorrow (see Isa. 50:11). They are without any feeling that they are sinners, without conviction, without conversion. So it was with the Pharisee who prayed, 'God, I thank thee, that I am not as other men are, extortioners, unjust, adulterers, or even as this publican. I fast twice in the week, I give tithes of all that I possess' (Luke 18:11-12). None can enter heaven on the ground of his own righteousness: 'Except your righteousness shall exceed the righteousness of the scribes and Pharisees, ye shall in no case enter into the kingdom of heaven' (Matt. 5:20). He must strip off his garments of self-righteousness. That was what Paul did when he said, 'I count all things but loss for the excellency of the knowledge of Christ Jesus my Lord' (Phil. 3:8).

3. Many will adopt sentiments which will effectually prevent the necessary preparation for heaven

Many deny the necessity of regeneration. They intend to live moral lives, and do not believe in the necessity of a change of heart. But all who seek to enter heaven without being born again will be disappointed. However sincere a person may be in disbelieving the doctrine, however much he may do to enter heaven without being born again, it makes no difference. The error must be fatal. The Saviour has repeatedly declared, 'Verily, verily, I say unto thee, Except a man be born again, he cannot see the kingdom of heaven' (John 3:3; cf. 3:5,7). After all that may be said to explain away this doctrine, it will be found to be of such pressing necessity that without it none can enter heaven.

This, by the way, is one gate which sinners are to enter. Repentance is the gate, and the only gate, which leads to the door of heaven. Sinners are commanded to 'strive', to 'agonize' and to 'enter' this gate. Those who deny the necessity of regeneration may seek to enter heaven, but they never seek to enter the strait gate. It is the command of Christ: 'Enter ... in at the strait gate' (Matt. 7:13).

The difficulty of repentance is stated as the reason why many will not be saved: 'Because strait is the gate, and narrow is the way, which leadeth unto life, and few there be that find it' (Matt. 7:14). Those who do not believe in regeneration do not even seek to enter in at the strait gate. All who attempt to climb up some other way will certainly be excluded (John 10:1). They spend their time in idle attempts to widen the gate. Instead of humbling themselves and breaking off their sins and striving to enter by regeneration and repentance, they waste their day of salvation by cutting and carving and widening the gate so that all may enter, with all their sins.

4. They do not seek at the right time

Many will seek to enter heaven, but their exertions will be too late. 'Afterward came also the other virgins, saying, "Lord, Lord, open to us." But he answered and said, "Verily I say unto you, I know you not" ' (Matt. 25:11-12). 'When once the master of the house is risen up, and hath shut to the door, and ye begin to stand without, and to knock at the door, saying, "Lord, Lord, open unto us"; and he shall answer and say unto you, "I know not whence ye are... I tell you, I know not whence ye are; depart from me, all ye workers of iniquity" ' (Luke 13:25-27).

Those who have frequently stilled their convictions and resisted the Spirit of God are in danger of being too late: 'Because I have called, and ye refused; I have stretched out my hand, and no man regarded' (Prov. 1:24). Then take heed 'lest there be any ... as Esau, who for one morsel of meat sold his birthright. For ye know how that afterward, when he would have inherited the blessing, he was rejected: for he found no place of repentance, though he sought it carefully with tears' (Heb. 12:16-17).

But hear the Saviour's word:
'Strive for the heavenly gate'.
Many will call upon the Lord,
And find their cries too late.

5. They are not willing to part with all for heaven

This was the case with the young man in the Gospel. He came to Christ with the important question: 'Good Master, what shall I do to inherit eternal life?' He imagined that he was willing to do anything to obtain heaven. 'Go and sell all that you have.' This tested him; it showed him his heart. It sent him away sad (Luke 18:18-23). It is recorded of Herod that when he heard John he 'did many things' (Mark 6:20).

With respect to the sinner anxious for his soul, doubtless, some particular sin prevents him from yielding to the terms of the gospel. Whatever it may be, the sinner must renounce it. He must break off from every sin — it is required of him to do it, on pain of eternal death: 'If any man will come after me, let him deny himself, and take up his cross daily, and follow me' (Luke 9:23). 'If thy right eye offend thee, pluck it out, and cast it from thee: for it is profitable for thee that one of thy members should perish, and not that thy whole body should be cast into hell' (Matt. 5:29). He must part with all his sins, or he must part with heaven. All who seek to enter heaven without renouncing all their sins seek in vain.

Or it may be some friend or acquaintance with whom the sinner is not willing to part, or whom he cannot bear to offend: ' "Let me first go bid them farewell, which are at home at my house." ... No man, having put his hand to the plough, and looking back, is fit for the kingdom of God' (Luke 9:61,62).

6. Some seek for a time and then drop the subject

This is often the case in times of revival. For a time they are alarmed; they read and attempt to pray. They struggle with conviction for a while. But they find their hearts so hard, and the duties of religion so troublesome and painful that they drop the subject; they give it up — and are lost for ever.

Those who are about to give it up commonly do so by taking offence. They take offence at almost anything. Thus it was in the time of Christ. They followed him for a while, but by and by his preaching came too close. Then hearts that had not been humbled could not endure it. They took offence and 'From that time many of his disciples went back, and walked no more with him' (John 6:66).

The inferences to be drawn from all this

1. The danger of loose sentiments on the subject of religion

If 'Strait is the gate...', let us beware how we attempt to widen it. We may succeed in quieting conscience, but we do so at the peril of losing our souls. No one will be better than the sentiments which he adopts will make him. What some call 'liberality' the Bible would pronounce 'unbelief'. No preacher ever made the way to heaven more difficult than the Son of God, who said, 'Wide is the gate, and broad is the way, that leadeth to destruction, and many ... go in thereat' (Matt. 7:13), and 'Strive to enter in at the strait gate: for many, I say unto you, will seek to enter in, and shall not be able' (Luke 13:24). If any preacher attempts to show an easier way to heaven than by the strait gate and narrow way of regeneration, you may know that he does not preach the way of salvation.

2. A warning

If this is so, then those who are not yet anxious for their souls may fear that they should yet be among that number. My friends, I must tell you that your fears are not without foundation. Many whose souls are as precious as yours have been lost, many who have been as anxious, many who have done more in religion. It is altogether uncertain how it will terminate. There is no safety here. You may after all lose your concern, and the last state will be worse than the first. And if you drop the duty, or quit now without a new heart, this will certainly be the case.

3. It is not surprising that some turn back even in times of revival

If many seek to enter in and shall not be able to do so, it would not be surprising if some of those who profess conversion during a revival should before long turn back. A revival is well described in the parable of several kinds of hearers — represented by thorns by the wayside, stony places, good ground. Those who have stood on the sidelines during a time of revival may be waiting to see how others stay the course. But even if a number of those who think they have experienced conversion should turn back by and by, that will not disprove the reality of it in others. Because there was a Judas among the apostles, had Christ no true disciples? Because the seed fell on stony places, does it follow that none fell on good ground?

When one to whom this description applies drops the subject and goes back to the world, how common it is for the wicked to speak of it with an air of triumph: 'There goes one of your good Christians!' What does this prove? It proves, first, that you who speak in this manner have no religion. Secondly, it indicates that you are glad that others are going to hell with you. Thirdly, the more there are that turn back, the greater the probability that you too will be lost. If others have been deceived, you may well imagine there are only a few who are going to heaven. So much greater, then, the probability that you will be lost. Remember this only proves the truth of our text: 'Strait is the gate, and narrow is the way, which leadeth unto life, and few there be that find it' (Matt. 7:14)

Finally, if there are those who seek and yet remain unconverted, what will become of those who do not even seek, but do nothing? If those who are anxious for their souls are unconverted, what about those who remain indifferent? If those who pray are in many cases still unconverted, what about those who never pray at all? If some have started to flee to the city of refuge and yet turn back, what about those who have not taken alarm at all? If some even of those who have taken alarm need to be told, 'Escape for your life!' what about those who, after all, look back and become pillars of salt, or who are still sleeping in Sodom? (See Gen. 19:17-26).

Regeneration

'But as many as received him, to them gave he power to become the sons of God, even to them that believe on his name: which were born, not of blood, nor of the will of the flesh, nor of the will of man, but of God' (John 1:12-13).

The important and simple doctrine taught by these words is that those who receive Christ, who have power given them to become the sons of God and who believe on his name, are 'born ... of God'. In other words, every real Christian becomes one by a special exertion of almighty power to change his heart.

The phrase 'born of God', or 'begotten of God', so often used by the writers of the New Testament, is figurative. Its appropriateness, when applied to things of a spiritual nature, arises from the analogy which exists between the beginning of our natural and spiritual existence. Believers are the sons of God and this must be understood in a particular sense. All men equally receive their existence and natural faculties from the Creator, and in this sense are *all* the children of

God. But when the Scriptures apply the phrases 'sons of God' and 'children of God' to the saints by way of distinction, it must be to point out a relationship to God which is not common to all men. This relationship is of a wholly new and spiritual nature and God is the sole author of it; and by virtue of it they are his sons — they are said to be 'born of him', or 'begotten of him', in allusion to the relationship which exists between earthly parents and their children.

The object of this text is to deny that our relationship to God as his spiritual children is produced in any way other than by his own special and sovereign power. It was originally intended to oppose the prejudices of the Jews. For the common opinion was that all who could be counted as the children of Abraham were heirs of the divine promises and entitled to eternal life. This notion was uniformly opposed by Christ and his apostles. Leaving aside any attempt to ascertain the precise meaning of the phrases, 'not of blood, nor of the will of the flesh, nor of the will of man', I observe that there were three ways in which individuals came to be reckoned as children of Abraham: by regular descent, by unlawful connection and by adoption. Whatever the method, the Jews supposed that whoever became a child of Abraham must of course have also become a child of God. The celebrated Lightfoot supposes that the object of the Evangelist is to cut off the false hopes of the Jews, by denying that either method, or indeed any method, of becoming the children of Abraham would make them the children of God. Another birth is necessary, a new conferring of sonship from above. They must be born again — born of God. Whatever may be the particular meaning of the text, the obvious general impression from it, and the one designed to be made by the sacred writer, is that all other ways of becoming the sons of God are false and visionary, except that of being born of him. It was spoken to meet the prevailing prejudices of the day, and may now be used in the same manner.

Of all subjects, that which represents change from death unto life is certainly one of the most important and interesting to us. To have clear and definite ideas here is of great moment. Error on such a fundamental point is awfully perilous.

In one sense all things are of God. He is the Creator and governor of all. All a man's powers and faculties are from God, and all the means of grace and institutions of religion are ordained by him. But when the Scriptures speak of being 'born of God', they mean something more than that a man is influenced by these means and institutions in the use of his ordinary powers and faculties.

To prevent misunderstandings, I have said that regeneration is the special work of almighty power. Advocates of erroneous doctrine have never dared to deny, directly, that saints are born of God, because this would be to renounce all appearance of belief in the Scriptures. They have chosen a surer method of propagating their views. While they retain the language of the sacred writers, they have attacked and frittered away their meaning until regeneration becomes the mere application of an external rite, or a persuasion of mind brought about in an ordinary manner, and a consequent reformation of morals.

False ideas concerning regeneration

To expunge error serves to illustrate the truth. I shall briefly consider some false notions respecting regeneration and then proceed to illustrate what it is to be born of God.

It is not baptism, or some external rite

I need not waste time in labouring to prove that baptism is not regeneration. Nothing is plainer than that an external rite cannot change the heart. Baptism is only a sign, or token, of the saving influences of the Holy Spirit, and is not that work itself. It cannot be the token of a thing and the thing itself at the same time. Both the Scriptures and experience show that all who are baptized are not regenerated, for in their lives and conduct many who are baptized are no different from the world which 'lieth in wickedness' (1 John 5:19). On this subject, I shall only add the words of an eminent English divine. 'This scheme,' says he, speaking of regeneration by water baptism, 'is the utter rejection and overthrow of the grace of our Lord Jesus Christ.' Again, he says, 'The vanity of this presumptuous folly is destructive of the grace of the gospel, invented to countenance men in their sins and to hide from them the necessity of being born again; and therein of turning unto God. But, my beloved Christian brethren, you have not so learned Christ.'

The absurdity of substituting this and other things of a like nature is so palpable and gross that it is very likely to be seen and apprehended where any considerable degree of knowledge respecting the nature of religion exists. There is far less danger from such extravagant notions than from those which are more specious and imposing.

The errors of Pelagius

Pelagius, in the fourth century, first invented and advocated a scheme of regeneration which, with a few modifications, sometimes in the phraseology, and sometimes by partial additions or diminutions, has been the scheme adopted by the great body of all the movements who have dissented from orthodox evangelical sentiments. Authors have appeared in different periods and in various countries who have brought forward this specious scheme of the new birth, as principally illustrated, or defined by themselves; and many whose reading is superficial have been deceived into supposing this view to be correct. The fact is that almost the whole system of vague and inadequate notions on this great subject is only the heresy of Pelagius, so universally condemned by the ancient church, which has now been newly dressed up, after the modern fashion, to secure a better reception.

The fundamental teachings of the Pelagian and Arminian scheme (for the two are in substance the same) are these:

> 1. That God not only proclaims the offers of grace and salvation to all men alike, but that the Holy Spirit is equally and sufficiently distributed to *all* men to ensure their salvation, provided they duly take advantage of the benefits bestowed upon them.
>
> 2. That the precepts and promises of the gospel are not only good and desirable in themselves, but so suited to the natural reason and interests of mankind that they will naturally be inclined to receive them, unless overpowered by prejudice and a habitually sinful way of life.
>
> 3. That the consideration of the threatenings and promises of the gospel is sufficient to remove these prejudices and reform that way of life.
>
> 4. That those who thus seriously reflect and amend their lives have the promise of the Holy Spirit and are entitled to the benefits of the new covenant.

Under this specious statement of fundamental principles, which is apt to strike a mind not given to deep consideration in a favourable manner, the very life and soul of gospel truth are taken away. According to this scheme, all men are regenerated alike, originally — all having an equal measure of the Spirit — and the difference between one man and another is to be ascribed wholly to himself, to the use he has made of the blessings vouchsafed to him. And regeneration is a reformation of life, induced by moral influences, or commenced in consequence of the understanding being enlightened and the affections being moved by divine truth alone. If you ask, 'How does salvation proceed from divine grace on this plan?' the answer is that all the means of improvement are bestowed by God and that this is where we find the grace.

The whole scheme is simply this: God gives faculties and grace to all, and to all alike, and with this provision they work out their own salvation, being persuaded to do so by the promises and threatenings of the gospel. The dreadful mischief which this widespread and popular scheme has caused springs from its plausibility — from the fact that so much that appears to be true is mixed with so many great and dangerous errors.

That the Holy Spirit makes use of the Word and many other instruments to bring sinners to Christ, I have no doubt. But that men are *naturally* so inclined as to approve of and obey the precepts of the gospel, unless some specially sinful way of life or prejudice prevents them, contradicts the whole tenor of the gospel, in which it is a fundamental principle that by nature we are children of wrath, and that we are at enmity with God, blinded to the light of his truth and dead in trespasses and sins. That the Holy Spirit is communicated to all in a sufficient manner to save them entirely overthrows the idea of any special grace, and makes one man as much 'born of God' as another! Our text says that as many as 'received Christ, and believed on his name' were born of God. If that is so, others, who did not, were not born of God, and the lack of any distinguishing influences on the part of the Spirit cannot be maintained.

It is a great stumbling-block in the way of many that God should give more of his Spirit to one than to another. To remove this subject of prejudice, Pelagius, and multitudes ever since, maintained that all men receive gifts alike, and are equally provided with the means to work out their salvation. This effectually destroys the new birth, and makes it common to every man alike. On this view Judas had as much grace as Paul; Ahab, who sold himself to work wickedness, had as much as David, a man after God's own heart. All the difference between them was owing to the different manner in which they made use of their privileges.

I know such doctrine is agreeable to corrupt nature, and the ready reception it has met with ever since it was first preached proves how agreeable it is to human reason. But neither the Scriptures nor experience afford us any reason to believe it. I do not doubt that the Spirit of God strives with all men who are not reprobates. I fully admit it. I admit that the promises and threats of the gospel would be sufficient to persuade us to a holy life if our understandings were neither darkened, nor our affections depraved. But after admitting all this, I deny that common grace makes us the sons of God, or that we are persuaded to be Christians without any special divine influence, or that all men receive the same measure of the Spirit.

After all preparatory means, all the promises and threats of the gospel, all the operation of common grace and all exertions of unregenerate sinners, they must be born of God to become his children. There must be a new creation — a work accomplished by almighty power; a sovereign, special, supernatural act, like making a world, or raising the dead, as to the power exerted; and without such an act no one can ever see the kingdom of heaven. Persuasion is not sufficient to make men new creatures. If the Spirit operates on the minds of men merely by setting persuasive arguments or motives before them, however diverse or well adapted to this purpose these arguments may be, yet ultimately, it depends on the will of man whether any shall be regenerated or not. According to this scheme the glory of regeneration would belong to ourselves. It would be uncertain also whether Christ would have any spiritual seed, as it would ultimately depend upon the uncertain determination of each individual before whom the motives were set. This, then, contradicts the Scriptures. God does not confine his operations to setting motives of persuasion before men: 'Thy people shall be willing in the day of thy power' (Ps. 110:3).

Moral persuasion to a better life confers no new real, supernatural strength to the soul which may enable it so to live. No new taste, no new spiritual discernment springs from persuasion. If regeneration comes in this manner, then a man begets himself; he is born of himself; he makes himself to differ from others (cf. 1 Cor. 4:6-7). On this plan the Spirit of God has no more to do than Paul or Apollos.

Besides, this is not what we pray for; we do not pray that motives may be set before us to regenerate ourselves, but that God would change us, that he would create us anew. The ancient churches urged this prayer upon the heretics, who denied a supernatural work in regeneration, and they felt themselves to be under great pressure from without.

There is, then, only one way left for a creature dead in trespasses and sins to rise to life. This is by the power of

God, which gives him life, creates him anew. Observe in what language sacred writers have chosen to communicate their ideas on this subject: 'born of God', 'begotten of God', 'quickened' or 'made alive from the dead', 'created anew'. If someone says that this is figurative language, I agree that it is, but if the figures used are at all correct, the work of regeneration must be the commencement of a new spiritual existence. On any other grounds the language of the Scriptures is, of all books, the most fanciful, lacking in meaning and obscure.

You may suppose all the preparation, all the knowledge, motives, morality (in the common usage of the term) and unregenerate strivings that you like — after all of that there must still be a new creation; the dead must be made alive; believers must be born of God. The same energy which brought Christ from the dead — the exceeding great power of the living God — must perform the work. This is what the apostle states when he prays that we 'may know ... what is the exceeding greatness of his power [towards us] who believe, according to the working of his mighty power, which he wrought in Christ, when he raised him from the dead' (Eph. 1:18-20).

Indeed, my friends, where else can we look for the origin of such a change as makes believers pass from death to life, but to the omnipotence of the divine Spirit? Is it our *understanding* which accomplishes this change? But our understanding is darkened (Eph. 4:18). 'The natural man receiveth not the things of the Spirit of God ... neither can he know them' (1 Cor. 2:14). Is it our *will*? But we are prone to evil 'as the sparks fly upward' (Job 5:7). Our wills are perverse and rebellious. Is it our *strength*? Christ died for the ungodly who are 'without strength' (Rom. 5:6). We are not sufficient of ourselves to think a good thought (2 Cor. 3:5).

Is it our *merits*? We merit nothing but utter rejection. Is it *the ministers of God* who persuade us? Paul may plant and Apollos water, but God gives the increase (1 Cor. 3:6).

Every effort has been made by the ingenuity of man — by palpably erroneous schemes and by plausible ones — to wrest the glory of this work from the hands of the Spirit of God and claim the operation for ourselves, or at least to share in the honour of it. But, after all these attempts, its origin can be traced only to the free and sovereign grace and almighty power of God. The work is all his and the glory must, and will, for ever belong exclusively to him.

It is a doctrine supported by the great light of the Reformation, and by the pillars of the evangelical churches ever since, that regeneration is a physical work. And by this they mean there is an actual new creation, just as real as that when the world was created — that a new spiritual taste, or discernment, and principle are implanted by a sovereign creative operation, and not simply a new direction given to the old faculties. Such a work being proved, the whole system of evangelical truth — the doctrines of grace, of divine sovereignty, of election, of redemption only by Christ, of human depravity and others connected with them — all flow from it. There is one grand, harmonious and perfect system, and God is the sum, the substance and the glory of all.

My friends, I am fully aware of the difficulties incident to the doctrines here laid down. I know full well how ready the natural heart is both to oppose and misconstrue them. But if the Bible supports them, it is enough. Here our human reason must bow. Here our proud hearts must submit. Charge them with mystery, with inconsistency, with being unprofitable and you assail, not man, but God. Look on his Word and read. There it stands — and it is written in characters of light: 'which were born not of blood, nor of the will of the flesh, nor of the will of man, but of God'.

This is the only birth which can fit us for heaven: 'Except a man be born again, he cannot see the kingdom of God' (John 3:3). We may please our fancies, and gratify our self-righteousness, by adopting loose Pelagian sentiments on this subject; we may remonstrate against such absolute dependence on the grace of God as has now been advocated, but a new heart and a right spirit will ultimately be found to be so absolutely necessary that without them we must perish for ever.

Sinners entreated to be reconciled to God

'Now then we are ambassadors for Christ, as though God did beseech you by us: we pray you in Christ's stead, be ye reconciled to God' (2 Cor. 5:20).

Were an ambassador sent from a foreign power with a message addressed to us, we would all pay attention to what he had to say. But the message of an earthly head of state is not what you are now called upon to receive, but a message from the court of heaven. It is addressed to every impenitent sinner: 'Now then we are ambassadors for Christ, as though God did beseech you by us: we pray you in Christ's stead,' that you will heed the message and comply with its demands, the sum of which is: 'Be ye reconciled to God.'

The text contains a summary of the apostles' preaching, not only to the Corinthians, but to mankind generally. Wherever they went, this was their message to sinners: 'We pray you in Christ's stead, be ye reconciled to God.'

Let us consider the duty of an ambassador in delivering his message. His great business is to publish the treaty of peace and to set before sinners the terms of reconciliation. In doing this, he is bound inviolably to adhere to the instructions of his divine Master. From these instructions he must not depart in the least degree. He must 'justify the ways of God to man'. He must hold up the character of God as a holy and righteous Sovereign, who claims the love and obedience of all his subjects. He must hold up the character of the sinner as odious in the eyes of infinite purity, as a lost and guilty criminal under the condemning sentence of God's holy law. On the one hand, he must bring into view the glorious gospel, with all its moving invitations and promises of eternal peace and joy. On the other, he must bring into view the broken law and the wrath of God as 'revealed from heaven against all ungodliness and unrighteousness of men' (Rom. 1:18), and point the sinner to the regions of despair and never-ending torments in hell. By the mercies of God, he must beseech, and by the terrors of the Lord he must endeavour to persuade men to be reconciled to God.

'As though God did beseech you by us.' Here mark the divine condescension. God beseeches. By whom? By his faithful ambassadors. Does *God* beseech? Then the ambassador is not to deliver his message in the name of a mortal man, but in the name, and by the authority of, the living God. And thus he must come in the name of God and deliver his whole message, without regard either to the love or hatred of men. As the faithful ambassador who penned the words of the text says, 'Even so we speak; not as pleasing men, but God, which trieth our hearts' (1 Thess. 2:4). 'Do I seek to please men? For if I yet pleased men, I should not be the servant of Christ' (Gal. 1:10).

'We pray you in Christ's stead.' Here again you will mark the same condescension. Christ still retains his compassion for sinners. He still pleads with them by his ambassadors, who are to stand and plead, beseeching hard-hearted rebels to be reconciled to God. This is their great business. It is all that they can do. I propose, first, to show what is implied in being reconciled to God.

1. What is implied in being reconciled to God

The Scriptures have decided this point with great clearness. It involves whatever is essential to the Christian character.

Firstly, it implies *a change from the state of an enemy to that of a friend.* All are by nature children of wrath, enemies, unreconciled to God. Hence it is asserted in the context: 'If any man be in Christ, he is a new creature: old things are passed away; behold, all things are become new' (2 Cor. 5:17). This is essential. Love is the distinguishing characteristic of friendship. Supreme love to God, for what he is in himself, is indispensable. 'Everyone that loveth is born of God, and knoweth God.' But 'He that loveth not knoweth not God; for God is love' (1 John 4:7,8). All, therefore, who have not been born of the Spirit are unreconciled. They still possess 'the carnal mind' which 'is enmity against God' (Rom. 8:7).

Secondly, reconciliation to God implies *love to his law*. This is a perfect transcript of his moral character. Love to God and love to his law are, therefore, essentially the same. 'Oh how love I thy law!' (Ps. 119:97). 'I delight in the law of God after the inward man' (Rom. 7:22). This is the language of a heart reconciled to God. And the person who is truly reconciled not only delights in the precepts of the law, but acquiesces in its penalty. Its condemning sentence appears to him to be right.

Thirdly, reconciliation to God implies *a willingness to accept salvation on the terms proposed in the gospel.* The satisfaction which Christ made on the cross is called a 'reconciliation' on the part of God. This, as committed to the apostles, is called the 'ministry' and 'word' of reconciliation (2 Cor. 5:18,19). Now those, and only those, who are pleased with the plan of salvation can be saved. The treaty of peace was formed in the counsels of eternity. God claims the right of prescribing the terms of reconciliation, without consulting the notions and feelings of men. That God should act in this manner is both just and merciful. It is just because God is the offended party, and man the offending party. It is surely improper for the condemned criminal to prescribe to his judge the terms on which he shall be pardoned. It is merciful because man, being a sinner justly condemned, has no claims to salvation on any terms whatever.

Hence we find that the Scriptures speak of God's 'reconciling the world unto himself' (2 Cor. 5:19) — not of his being reconciled to the world, or to their plans of salvation. But the fact that Christ has died, and that a way of salvation has been provided, does not settle the question whether the sinner will be saved. If he is displeased with the plan of salvation, and does not freely subscribe with his hand unto the Lord, instead of being saved he will fall under an even greater condemnation.

Mankind are naturally opposed to the gospel plan of salvation. If it were not so, why is there a single enemy to God among all those who have once heard the gospel? Why do not all at once comply with the terms of salvation? Why is there so much opposition to the doctrines of the gospel?

This subject explains the reason. Men are unreconciled to God. The fact that 'The carnal mind is enmity against God' accounts for all this opposition. That persons are opposed to the doctrines which they hear from the pulpit is no evidence that those doctrines are not true. A previous question remains to be settled. Are these persons reconciled to God? Have they been born again? If not, opposition is to be expected. If the unregenerate heart is not opposed to the truth, the Bible is not true. Corrupt sentiments will be pleasing to a corrupt heart. Show me a scheme of doctrines with which mankind are naturally pleased, and I will show you one that never came from heaven. The very fact that sinners are unreconciled to God implies that they are not pleased with the terms of reconciliation. If they were not opposed to these terms, there would be no necessity to beseech them to be reconciled. They would of course be reconciled.

That mankind are not reconciled to the terms of salvation is evident, not only from the conduct of thoughtless sinners, but from that of those who are awakened to a sense of their sin and danger. One would suppose that the gospel of reigning grace and the glad tidings of a Saviour would be embraced with the utmost readiness by such sinners — that they would at once individually exclaim in transports of joy, 'This is the Saviour I want! This is the salvation suited to my condition!' But, alas! even the convicted sinner, however clearly he may see his lost condition, and however great his distress may be, will not come to Christ that he might have life (John 5:40). He continues to enquire, 'What must I do to be saved?' and the gospel answer, 'Repent and believe on the Lord Jesus Christ,' gives him no relief. His proud heart will not submit to these terms. But let such people remember that the terms of salvation will never be altered. The sinner must repent or perish.

2. A plea to the reader to be reconciled to God

Having shown what is implied in being reconciled to God, I proceed to beseech all those reading these pages who are as yet impenitent to be thus reconciled.

My business now lies directly with those who are the enemies of God, for only they need to be reconciled. An enemy to God — where can the individual be found, on whom God has fastened this charge? The text takes it for granted that *all* to whom the gospel is sent are in a state of enmity to God. The King of heaven would not send his ambassadors to his faithful subjects, to beseech them to be reconciled to their Friend whom they supremely love. But multitudes who yield some general assent to the truths of the gospel are not convinced that they have any need to be reconciled to God. Many assert that they never were his enemies, that they were always reconciled to him. If this is so, they are not lost and Christ has nothing to do with them, for he came 'to seek and to save that which was lost' (Luke 19:10).

Numbers who have long imagined themselves at peace with God have only been 'at ease in Zion' (see Amos 6:1). This was the case of the great body of the Jewish nation and of Paul himself, who 'after the ... straitest sect of [their] religion ... lived a Pharisee', until he was awakened by the voice of the Son of God saying, 'Saul, Saul, why persecutest thou me?' (Acts 26:5,14). And of his brethren the Israelites he says, 'I bear them record that they have a zeal of God, but not according to knowledge' (Rom. 10:2). It was over the case of such people that he wept: 'For many walk, of whom I have told you often, and now tell you even weeping, that they are the enemies of the cross of Christ' (Phil. 3:18).

And do you, dear reader, plead 'Not guilty'? No child of Adam can stand up before his Judge and say, 'I am innocent.' All the subjects of divine grace were once unreconciled to God and 'were by nature the children of wrath, even as others' (Eph. 2:3). 'You, that were sometime alienated and enemies in your mind by wicked works, yet now hath he reconciled' (Col. 1:21).

Have you become reconciled to God? You have seen what is implied in becoming reconciled. It implies a change from the state of an enemy to that of a friend. Are you conscious of having experienced such a change? Do you now hate what you once loved, and love what you once hated? Do you delight in communion with God? Is the language of your heart, 'Whom have I in heaven but thee? And there is none upon earth that I desire beside thee'? (Ps. 73:25). Or is the thought of a present, holy, heart-searching God a terror to your mind? Do you cherish the secret wish that there were no God, that you might sin without restraint? Do you dismiss, as much as possible, serious thoughts from your mind, that you may enjoy the pleasures of sin undisturbed?

Love to the divine law is another evidence of reconciliation. 'If a man love me,' says Christ, 'he will keep my words' (John 14:23). 'This is the love of God, that we keep his commandments: and his commandments are not grievous' (1 John 5:3). Do you love God's law, and strive to obey it? Or do you live in the neglect of known duty? Do you murmur at the strictness of the law and find more delight in forbidden paths that in walking in the strait and narrow way to life? Do you cast off fear and restrain prayer? Are you ashamed to confess Christ before men? Are you more anxious to secure the friendship of the world than the approbation of God? If so, there can be no doubt as to your true character and conditions. 'Whosoever ... will be a friend of the world is the enemy of God' (James 4:4).

Reconciliation to God, as we have seen, implies also a willingness to accept salvation on the terms which God proposes. Are you pleased with the terms of salvation? If you are, you have doubtless complied with them. Have you repented and believed in Christ? If not, why? No reason can be assigned but the opposition of your heart. If you were pleased with the terms of salvation, you would not remain in impenitence and unbelief another moment.

Many, I am aware, express strong desires for salvation and sometimes say they would give all the world, if they had it, for an interest in the divine favour, while they have never found it in their hearts to feel the least degree of contrition for their sins, or the least degree of love and gratitude to the God who made them and the Saviour who died for them. Whatever value such individuals may place on a heaven of eternal happiness, they do actually prefer sin to everything else; and in spite of the offers of eternal life, the calls of a crucified Saviour, the invitations, commands and threatenings of Almighty God, they are now forcing their way down to eternal perdition.

Let me ask you again, have you become reconciled to God?

To all who do not love God supremely, delight in his law and render cheerful obedience to its precepts, and who do not acknowledge the justice of its penalty and weep over their unreasonable transgressions — to all who are not willing to be saved on the humbling terms of the gospel and to enlist under the Redeemer's banner, and who do not rejoice that the Lord reigns, I have a message from God. It is a case of life and death to your souls, and as such I beseech you to regard it.

What now is the cause of this enmity between you and God? Has God ever injured you? Has he ever dealt unkindly with you? What have you to allege against his character, against his law, or against this treaty of peace?

Do you ask what God requires of you? The answer is plain: 'Be … reconciled to God.' This is what God claims. And from this we cannot depart without entering on forbidden ground. He claims the heart. And from this we cannot depart without disloyalty to God. Individuals and nations may negotiate a treaty of peace, though the heart may not be engaged. An outward reconciliation may be effected while the heart remains the same. But not so with God. He looks on the heart. If that is withheld, ' "To what purpose is the multitude of your sacrifices unto me?" saith the Lord?' (Isa. 1:11). If the heart is not engaged, however much sinners may speak about wanting a reconciliation, their insolence is met with this impulsive demand: 'Who hath required this at your hand?' (Isa. 1:12). Without this, not a step can be taken towards settling your peace with God.

And now all things are ready and God is inviting and beseeching you to accept his mercy? What is the reply of your heart? Do you not like the terms of this treaty? You are required only to be 'reconciled to God'. What can be more reasonable than this? Is it hard that you should be required to love God, to feel sorrow for sin, to confess and forsake it? Is this hard? Or is sin so lovely and so desirable that it appears hard and unreasonable that you should be required to hate and oppose it with all your heart? Why, then, will you not renounce it? Is sin so noble a thing in itself and so desirable in its consequences that you cannot part with it, that you will lay down your life — your eternal life, for its sake? Your love of sin is all the excuse you have, or can have.

Or will you plead your inability? What! You cannot be reconciled to God, cannot feel sorrow for sin, cannot cease to rebel against the King of heaven! What an acknowledgement this is! Out of your own mouth you will be condemned. If, indeed, you are so opposed to God that you cannot feel sorrow for sin, this is the very reason why you ought to be condemned. The harder it is for you to repent and love God, the more wicked you are, and the greater will be your condemnation.

God himself is beseeching you to be reconciled. And why do you not obey? Have your pride and stubbornness risen to such a pitch that you will not do the most reasonable thing, even though God himself beseeches you?

In the name of God I beseech you to 'be reconciled'. Why will you stand out against the will of heaven? You are on the side of his enemies. The prince of darkness, ever since his first rebellion, has been attempting to rear his kingdom within the limits of Jehovah's empire. But how feeble are all his attempts! 'He that sitteth in the heavens shall laugh: the Lord shall have them in derision' (Ps. 2:4). 'The Lord hath prepared his throne in the heavens; and his kingdom ruleth over all' (Ps. 103:19). Why, then, will you continue this unequal contest with your God? He is the rightful Sovereign of the universe, and claims a throne in every heart. You are under infinite obligations to him as your Creator and constant preserver, and are therefore bound to obey him.

God possesses all excellence in himself, and on this account he deserves the supreme love of all his rational creatures. It is the duty even of the fallen angels to love him, for their rebellion has not cancelled their obligations. While God is on the throne, all his enemies, whether on earth or in hell, will be for ever criminal for not loving him, whatever torments they may endure. For on what principle can the prince of darkness justify his conduct in maintaining eternal war with the King of heaven? But while you continue unreconciled to God you virtually justify all the rebellion of wicked men and devils. And are you willing to be the apologists of the devil and his angels?

Again, consider what God has done for your salvation. The gift of a Saviour was not an act of justice to our world. Sinners had no right to demand the blood of the Son of God to atone for their guilt. Why then should he come to our world with a message of peace? Why not take on himself the nature of angels and extend pardoning mercy to those of them who had fallen? Though this has not been done, they are not justified in continuing in rebellion against God. No more would man have man been justified, if Christ had never died.

But let us suppose that Christ had left the race of Adam and gone down to redeem the fallen angels, should we not have been astonished at the mercy of God to them? And if those rebels had mocked and insulted the beloved Son of God and, in their hellish rage, had stripped him, crowned him with thorns, nailed him to the cross and put him to death — would we not have thought this to be wickedness that flies in the face of heaven? What depravity, I ask you, would this conduct have manifested to the universe?

How much more astonishing, then, that this Saviour has concluded a treaty of peace for rebellious man and now sends this message to you: 'Be ... reconciled to God!'

In his name I plead. You may disregard the words of a dying fellow mortal. Let him be forgotten. But will you not pay heed to the voice of God? 'Hear, O heavens, and give ear, O earth, for the Lord hath spoken!' (Isa. 1:2). His commanding word to every sinner who reads these words is:

'Be ... reconciled to God.' Have you not continued long enough in your rebellion? Have you not resisted his call long enough? And will you now again turn away from him who speaks from heaven? Will you not heed the voice of the one from heaven who speaks such gracious words — the Saviour who shed his blood? Have you no repentance — not a tear to shed for the sins which nailed him to the cross?

Oh, what amazing love invites you! He is 'the brightness of [the Father's] glory, and the express image of his person' (Heb. 1:3) — and is he unworthy of your love?

He is the delight of the Father — his only begotten Son, in whom he is well pleased — and is he unworthy of your love?

He is the Lamb of God, the light of the heavenly world, and receives the homage of angels and glorified spirits — and is he unworthy of your love?

When, from his exalted throne, he beheld the miserable enemies of God sitting in the region and shadow of death, he left his Father's side and, with the keys of death and hell at his command, passed by the fallen angels, opened the doors of rebellious man's prison and lit up his dreary abode with rays of celestial hope — and is he unworthy of your love?

Admiring angels, eager to bear the news of his entrance into our world, announced to the shepherds the birth of their incarnate God and sang, 'Glory to God in the highest, and on earth peace, good will toward men' (Luke 2:14) — and is he unworthy of your love?

He was 'a man of sorrows, and acquainted with grief' (Isa. 53:3). He knew no sin, neither was guile found in his mouth (2 Cor. 5:21; 1 Peter 2:22). Yet he was treated as a stranger and an outcast — as one who was unfit to live.

'The world knew him not' (John 1:10). 'Foxes have holes, and the birds of the air have nests; but [the Saviour had] not where to lay his head' (Matt. 8:20). He was esteemed as being less worthy to live than the vilest robber. Barabbas may live, but he must die. He was stoned, and found no rest in his passage through this world, He was falsely accused, unjustly condemned, flogged, arrayed in a purple robe, crowned with thorns; a vast multitude of feeble worms hailed him with acclamations of mock homage; they spat upon him, struck him with the palms of their hands and nailed him to the cross. There he yielded up his spirit. But he rose from the dead and ascended to his throne of glory, from where he now invites you to his arms and beseeches you to accept the salvation which he has purchased with his blood — and is he unworthy of your love?

'If any man love not the Lord Jesus Christ, let him be Anathema Maranatha' (1 Cor. 16:22).

I must close my feeble entreaties and leave the outcome with God. This is, perhaps, the only time that I shall address you, in the name of God, on this side of the eternal world. Sinners, must I leave you where I found you, unreconciled to God? Your business is not with a fellow mortal. I have done, and the whole remains to be settled between God and your souls. However hard you may think this message, it is not mine. God beseeches — God *commands* your compliance *now*. And will you raise your feeble arm to oppose? God is on the throne — and have you an arm like God's? However opposed you may be, yet God is on the throne — and what can you do? God is on the throne, and will dash his enemies in pieces like a potter's vessel (Ps. 2:9).

Before I close, I must your remind you, that for some who read these pages this may be the last call — the last offer of peace — which God will ever send you. But a different message will soon arrive. You will shortly hear again from your offended Sovereign. Before the setting of the sun, the messenger of death may be despatched with a commission to drag some guilty soul to his dread tribunal. He may even now be at the door.

By the mercies of God, and by the terrors of his wrath, by the joys of heaven and the pains of hell, by the merits of a Saviour's blood and by the worth of your immortal soul, I beseech you — lay down the arms of your rebellion; bow and submit to your rightful Sovereign. Oppose, and still he will reign. For God has set his King upon his holy hill of Zion, and has sworn by himself that unto him every knee shall bow (Ps. 2:6; Isa. 45:23; Phil. 2:10).

Once he came to earth with a message of peace and good will to men. But shortly he will be 'revealed from heaven with his mighty angels, in flaming fire taking vengeance on them that know not God, and that obey not the gospel of our Lord Jesus Christ: who shall be punished with everlasting destruction from the presence of the Lord, and from the glory of his power' (2 Thess. 1:8-9).